# Acid Rain

## Louise Petheram

FRANKLIN WATTS
LONDON•SYDNEY

© 2002 Franklin Watts

First published in 2002 by
Franklin Watts
96 Leonard Street
London
EC2A 4XD

Franklin Watts Australia
56 O'Riordan Street
Alexandria
NSW 2015

ISBN: 0 7496 4482 6
Dewey Decimal Classification 363.73
A CIP catalogue reference for this book is available
from the British Library

Printed in Dubai

Editor: Kate Banham
Designer: Mark Mills
Art Direction: Jonathan Hair
Illustration: Ian Thompson
Picture Research: Diana Morris
Consultant: Sally Morgan, Ecoscene

Photo acknowledgements
The publishers would like to thank the following for their permission
to reproduce photographs in this book.

Greg Abel/Environmental Images: 9bl; Martin Bond/Environmental Images: 28t;
Andrew Brown/Ecoscene: 9t, 17t; Graham Burns/Environmental Images: 11br; John
Corbett/Ecoscene: 12t; Corbis: 23t; Colin Cuthbert/SPL: 8t; Stephen Dalton/NHPA: 19t;
Ecoscene: fr cover, 22b; Mark Edwards/Still Pictures: 6t, 19b; Mary Evans PL: 10b;
Mark Fallander/Environmental Images: 14cl; © FSC: 17b; Dylan Garcia/Still Pictures:
27b; Don Gray/Photofusion: 15t; Nick Hawkes/Ecoscene: 14tr; Mike Jackson/Still
Pictures: 5tl; Jonathan Kaplan/Still Pictures: 14-15b; Yoram Lehmann/Still Pictures: 11tr;
Charlotte MacPherson/Environmental Images: 16b; Chris Martin/Environmental
Images: 4c; Rick Miller/Agstock/SPL: 20-21; Sally Morgan/Ecoscene: 17c; Eddie
Mulholland/Reuters/Popperfoto: 11bl; Juan Carlos Munoz/Still Pictures: 7t; Trevor
Perry/Environmental Images: 12-13b, 21bl; Melanie Peters/Ecoscene: 29c; Ray Pforter/
Still Pictures: 22tl; Richard Pike/Still Pictures: 26b; Charlie Pye-Smith: 28-29; Harmut
Schwarz/Still Pictures: 23c; R. Sorensen & J.Olsen/NHPA: 18t; Tek Image/SPL: 25t;
Wolk-UNEP/Still Pictures: 4-5b.

# Contents

Words printed in *italic* are explained in the glossary.

# The present situation

Scientific research has shown that acid rain has harmed the environment in some places. The word acid comes from the Latin 'acidus' meaning sour. Foods like lemon juice and vinegar are acids. Acid rain is rain that is more acidic than normal.

## Agricultural problems

Most plants have a particular type of environment where they grow best. Farmers grow varieties of plants best suited to the climate and soil in their area. Acid rain falling in an area can change the environment, so the plants do not grow as well. Poor tree growth in some European and American forests was one of the early signs that told scientists that acid rain was a problem. Acid rain can also change the water in lakes and streams so fish do not grow as well.

Damage to trees was one of the first signs of the acid rain problem.

## Damage to buildings

Acid rain or acid pollution *erodes*, or wears away, anything made of stone or metal. Bridges and railway lines are weakened and need repairing or replacing earlier than they would without acid rain. The metal bodywork of cars and other vehicles rusts more quickly, so the vehicles do not last as long. Ancient stone monuments and buildings are worn away by the acid rain falling on them. Decorative carvings become less clear. Eventually they disappear unless replaced with new stone.

Acid rain makes vehicles rust more quickly.

Acid pollution makes breathing problems worse.

# Poor health

Some acid pollution takes the form of acidic particles in the air. When people breathe them in these particles damage the lungs. This causes breathing difficulties and illnesses such as asthma. For people who already have breathing problems, this pollution makes them worse, and can cause death. In some areas this can mean that people are less healthy and need more time off work and school, and that more money is needed for hospitals and medicines.

## ◆ How you can help

There is a clear link between acid rain and the fuel used in *industry*. Helping industry use less fuel will reduce acid rain damage. You can help by doing simple things such as walking to school if possible, turning lights out when you leave a room, turning the central heating down a little and switching off computers when you've finished using them.

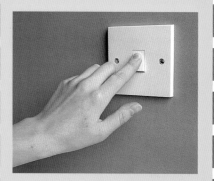
Using less energy would help to solve the acid rain problem.

# What is acid rain?

The atmosphere makes it possible for water and acid pollution to move around as clouds and rain.

Our Earth is surrounded by a mixture of gases called the atmosphere. The atmosphere also contains tiny dust particles and polluting gases, which can dissolve in the water vapour and fall in the rain. If the dissolved gases and particles that make the rain are more acid than normal it is called acid rain.

## How acid rain is caused

Pure water is not an acid, but even clean rainwater is slightly acidic. This is because it has carbon dioxide from the air dissolved in it. Rain is only called 'acid rain' if it is more acid than normal. The main causes of acid rain are gases called sulphur dioxide ($SO_2$) and nitrogen oxides (NOx). These dissolve in the water in the atmosphere to make acids. Bright sunlight speeds up the process. This makes the acid rain problem worse.

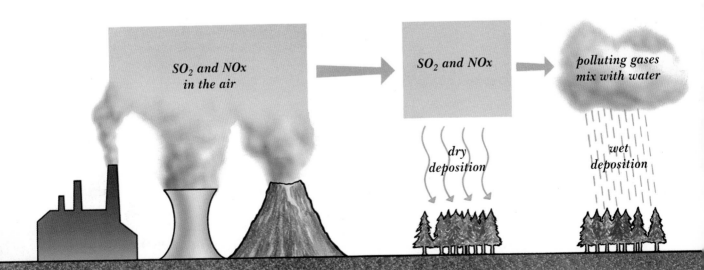

$SO_2$ and NOx in the air

$SO_2$ and NOx

polluting gases mix with water

dry deposition

wet deposition

# Natural acid rain

Although most acid rain is caused by human activities, some acid rain occurs naturally. Erupting volcanoes give off smoke containing water vapour, carbon dioxide, sulphur dioxide and nitrogen compounds. The sulphur dioxide and nitrogen compounds cause small amounts of acid rain near the volcano.

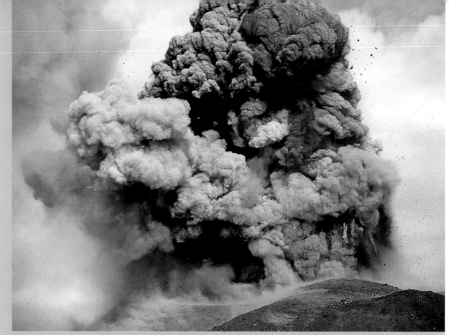

**Erupting volcanoes give off gases that cause acid rain.**

# Acid deposition

*Acid deposition* is anything acidic that comes down to the ground out of the air. Dry acid deposition is acid gases and particles. These make up about half the acid landing on the Earth. Acid rain is wet acid deposition. It includes rain, snow and fog that is more acid than normal. Acid rain soaks into the ground making the soil acidic. Dry acid deposition can make the soil acidic too. Wind blows the acid gases and particles on to buildings, vehicles and so on. Later rainwater washes the particles down into the soil.

## ◆ Sustainable solution

Vehicle exhaust fumes contain large amounts of nitrogen oxides and some sulphur dioxides. Much has been done to reduce these. Since 1983 in the United States, and 1993 in Europe, new cars have been fitted with catalytic converters that reduce the amount of nitrogen oxides. Fuel companies have improved fuels so that they contain less sulphur and burn more completely. There are laws to measure and control the amount of harmful gases given out by vehicles.

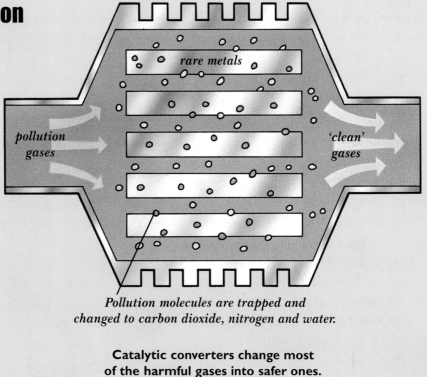

*Pollution molecules are trapped and changed to carbon dioxide, nitrogen and water.*

**Catalytic converters change most of the harmful gases into safer ones.**

# Measuring acid rain

Strong acids can damage a wide range of different materials. Scientists are able to measure the acidity of rain and particles in the air. This helps them find out where the acid pollution is coming from, and estimate how much damage it will cause.

Scientists can use pH meters to measure how acidic the rain is.

## Using pH numbers

*pH numbers* tell scientists how acidic or alkaline something is. Alkaline substances are the opposite of acids. Alkalis can be mixed with acids to neutralise them. pH 1 is an extremely strong acid, 7 is neutral (neither acid or alkali), 14 is an extremely strong alkali. Your digestive juices have a pH value of about 1.05–2.0, lemon juice is 2.3, clean rainwater about 6.5, blood 7.4 and toothpaste 9.9. Acid rain is usually defined as rainwater with a pH value of 5.5 or less. pH values can be measured with *indicator solutions* that change colour when they are put into different strength acids and alkalis. Scientists usually use pH meters.

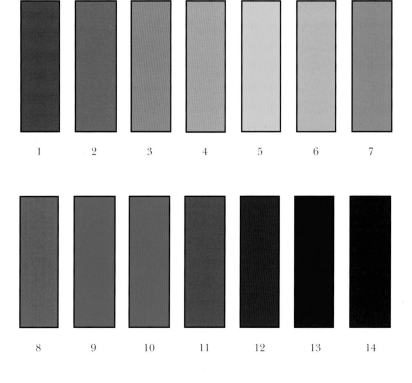

The colour of the indicator solution tells how acidic a substance is.

# Measuring atmospheric acidity

Scientists measure dry acid pollution by collecting air samples and testing them for a range of different harmful chemicals. They count the number of molecules of the chemical compared with the number of air molecules. The values are given as parts per million (ppm), that is the number of pollution molecules in one million air molecules. Scientists also collect samples of the rainwater and measure its acidity using a pH value meter or indicator.

Limestone and chalk rocks are naturally alkaline. They neutralise the effects of acid rain.

Air quality monitoring stations collect air samples and test them for polluting gases and other substances.

## Measuring the acidity of soil

When acid rain soaks into soil, it makes the soil acidic. You can buy simple testing kits that measure the soil's acidity by mixing a small amount of it with an indicator solution and observing the colour change. The acidity of soil is affected by the rocks making up the soil as well as by the rain falling on it. Soils that contain limestone rock are naturally alkaline. The alkaline rocks in these soils neutralise acid rain falling on the soil.

## ◆ Science in action

Collect rainwater samples from different places in your local area. Use Universal Indicator Paper (available from your school or from chemistry sets) to measure the acidity of the different rainwater samples. How acidic is the rain? Does it vary in different places locally? If it does, can you suggest any reasons why this might be?

# What causes acid rain?

All activities that burn fossil fuel cause some acid rain.

Burning fuels causes acid rain. Most of our fuels are still *fossil fuels* formed from plants and animals that died many millions of years ago. A lot of these fossil fuels release sulphur dioxide and nitrogen oxides when they are burnt, and these gases cause acid rain. Several things affect the amount of acid rain caused, such as the type of fossil fuel used and how completely it is burnt.

## The history of acid rain

Acid rain began with the Industrial Revolution in about 1750, when steam power began to be used to drive machinery. This was when large amounts of fossil fuels began to be burnt to produce energy. The problem of acid rain became gradually worse, until, in the last decades of the 20th century, scientists began to observe widespread *environmental damage*. Since the acid rain problem was discovered a number of changes have been put in place to try to prevent further damage to the environment and to undo the existing damage.

The problem of acid rain began with chimneys like these in the Industrial Revolution.

# Industry and cars

Both motor vehicles and industries, such as power stations and furnaces, have been blamed for causing acid rain. Studies in the United States have shown that over two-thirds of the sulphur dioxide in the atmosphere is produced by power stations that burn fossil fuels, and by industrial and domestic furnaces and boilers. These sources also produce half of the nitrogen oxides. Motor vehicles using petrol or diesel produce almost all the rest of the nitrogen oxides.

Coal-burning industries produce most of the sulphur dioxide. Motor vehicles produce almost half the nitrogen oxides.

# Scientific research

The chemical reactions that take place in the atmosphere to produce acid rain are very complicated. At first many industries demanded more research, arguing that there was no proof that they were really to blame for acid rain. Governments tended to agree with the industries, because it was expensive to reduce the amount of pollution. Since the 1980s however, governments and industries have worked together to introduce laws to reduce emissions that cause acid rain, and the damage it causes.

Politicians have an important part to play in reducing the emissions that cause acid rain.

## ◆Sustainable solution

Sulphur dioxide emissions from power stations are being reduced by using 'cleaner' coal. This coal contains less sulphur so gives off less sulphur dioxide when it burns. Devices called 'scrubbers' are fitted to chimneys to chemically remove the sulphur dioxide from the waste gases. Some power stations are changing to natural gas, which creates hardly any sulphur dioxide. Others use non fossil fuel technologies such as hydroelectric power, or solar power, which produce no sulphur dioxide at all.

Using wind power to generate electricity does not cause acid rain.

Acid rain is mostly caused by industrial activity and by vehicle exhausts. However, it is not only industrial areas that are affected by acid rain. Many of the worst affected areas are *rural areas* hundreds of kilometres from any industry.

**Some areas worst affected by acid rain are many kilometres from industrial areas.**

## How acid rain gases move around

Smoke particles are fairly heavy. They sink back to Earth near to their source. The gases and particles that cause acid rain are much lighter. They are carried large distances by air currents. In low wind speeds, or certain weather conditions that prevent the warm air rising, the polluting gases and particles stay near their source, causing problems there. In higher wind speeds they can be carried hundreds of kilometres from their source.

## The purpose of tall chimneys

Industry has used tall chimneys since long before people knew about acid rain. Tall chimneys release the smoke high into the atmosphere. By the time the smoke sinks back down to the ground it has spread over a large area. Because the smoke at ground level has thinned out so much, visibility and smells are improved, and fewer human respiratory problems are caused.

**Polluting gases spread much further from their source in high wind speeds.**

**Prevailing winds carry acid rain hundreds of kilometres from where it was created.**

*prevailing wind*

*rainwater with high acidity*

*rainwater with medium acidity*

● *country giving out more than one million tonnes of sulphur dioxide per year.*

# Where does the acid rain end up?

There are regular patterns of air flow around the Earth, known as prevailing winds. This means that most acid rain moves on a predictable path from its source to the area where it falls. Many forests in Central Europe have suffered acid rain damage caused partly by the activities of their neighbouring countries. Canadian scientists have estimated that about half the sulphur deposited as acid rain in Canada comes from sources in the United States.

## ◆ Science in action

Water currents and air currents behave in the same way. You can use currents in water to show the effect that air temperature has on polluting gases.

**You will need:** food colouring, 2 transparent jars, a drinking straw

Carefully mix some food colouring in hot water. This is your 'pollution'. Fill 2 transparent jars, one with hot water and one with cold water. Fill the drinking straw with 'pollution' by dipping it in the colouring and placing your finger over the end. Then, keeping the end of the straw sealed, take the straw to each of the jars of water and release a small amount of 'pollution' slowly into the bottom of each one. Does the 'pollution' move the same way in each jar?

# Threat to human health

Acid deposition can be in the form of dry acidic gases and particles in the air. All creatures, including humans, breathe in these particles when they breathe the polluted air. The damage this causes depends on how many harmful particles are in the air.

Here the air pollution is obvious, but a lot of the harmful particles in the air are invisible.

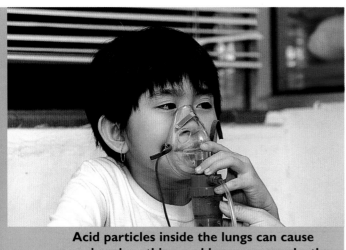
Acid particles inside the lungs can cause serious breathing problems or even death.

## The effects of breathing acid pollution

The sulphur dioxide and nitrogen oxide gases mix with oxygen, water and chemicals in the atmosphere. They form tiny acidic particles that are inhaled deep into the lungs. This makes the inside of the lungs sore and causes illnesses such as bronchitis and asthma. People can die from these illnesses and from related problems, such as heart disease, caused by the lung damage.

## Temperature inversions

The atmosphere usually gets colder the further you go above the Earth's surface. Warm air at ground level usually rises, taking any air pollution with it. *Temperature inversions* are weather conditions where the air at ground level is covered by a layer of warmer air higher up. In temperature inversions, the smog, a mixture of fog and pollution, cannot rise, and is trapped near the ground. In some cities, such as Mexico City and Tokyo, more people die from breathing problems when there is a temperature inversion.

These children are helping solve the problem of acid rain by walking to school safely with an adult instead of riding in cars or buses.

# Pollution in different areas

The threat to human health is greatest in areas where there are most particles of acid pollution in the air. This is usually in areas where a lot of industries burn fossil fuels, or with busy traffic. Research has shown that children living close to major roads are more likely to have asthma than children in rural areas. One difficulty scientists have is that other air pollutants, such as ozone, can also cause similar illnesses to acid pollution. Scientists have to work out how much illness is caused by the acid pollution, and how much by something else.

Pollution seems to float over some cities, looking like a layer of fog.

# Threat to forests

In 1984, reports said that almost half the trees in the Black Forest in Germany had been damaged by acid rain. Other studies soon reported similar damage in areas of the northern United States, Canada and parts of northern Europe.

## Forest damage

For years scientists had observed that forests in some areas grew more slowly than expected. Tree leaves or needles turned brown and fell off, while some trees died completely. Tests on the air, soil and water showed that what all these areas had in common was acid rain.

## How acid rain affects forests

Acid rain weakens trees by damaging leaves, but most damage is done by acid rain soaking into the soil. As the soil becomes more acidic, *nutrients* are dissolved and washed away. Sometimes *toxic substances* are released from the soil. Tree roots grow weaker, making the trees more likely to be damaged by disease, wind and cold weather.

The trees in this New York forest have lost needles and branches, and are dying because of the effects of acid rain.

# Acid rain and high altitude

The same amount of acid rain damages trees at *high altitude* more seriously than trees on lower ground. Scientists believe this is because trees at high altitude are often surrounded by clouds of acidic fog. This acid fog removes essential nutrients in the needles or leaves. The tree becomes weaker and is more likely to be killed by the colder temperatures that also exist at high altitude.

**Trees stop growing naturally at very high altitudes. Acid rain stops trees growing lower down mountains.**

# What areas are most affected?

Trees in some places seem able to survive acid rain better than trees growing in other places. This is because the amount of damage caused depends on the type of soil as well as on the amount of acid rain. If the soil is naturally acidic, the extra acidity caused by acid rain can be just enough to stop the trees growing. Trees in areas with thin soils also suffer more because the thin soil makes it harder for these trees to grow anyway. The acid rain can be just the extra problem that makes growth impossible.

**Some soils contain chalk or limestone that prevents the acid rain causing too much damage.**

## ◆ How you can help

The forests that suffer most damage are those where the trees are exposed to other problems as well as acid rain. By buying wood products with a Forest Stewardship Council (FSC) label, you are buying wood from trees grown in healthy forests, allowing forest environments damaged by acid rain the time they need to recover.

FSC

# Threat to water life

The beautiful clear blue colour of this Norwegian lake shows that very few plants or animals are living in the water because of acid rain damage.

Lakes and streams become acidic by acid rain falling on them, and by acid rain draining into them through the surrounding soils. Acid rain can also dissolve toxic chemicals from the soil and wash them into rivers and streams.

## Acid lakes

Most freshwater lakes and streams have a natural pH value of between 6 and 8. In June 2001 the United States Environmental Protection Agency reported that in some of the areas of North America, the pH level of many lakes was below 5, in one case as low as 4.2. In many freshwater lakes in Norway and Sweden, whole fish populations have been poisoned by aluminium ions released from the surrounding acidic soil. Many lakes and streams in mountain areas become acidic for a short while during storms and in spring. This is because they are filled by heavy rain or melting snow draining from surrounding hills. The extra acidity can kill fish and other *aquatic life*.

# Effect on aquatic environments

Even when fish and aquatic insects can survive the acidity and toxic chemicals washed out of the soil by acid rain, their growth is often affected. Adults are smaller, more likely to die from disease, and less likely to breed successfully. Even if they do breed, their young are more vulnerable to the acid levels than the adults. Most fish eggs will not hatch in water with a pH value of 5 or less. Species that are higher up the food chain than the dying species suffer, because some of their food has disappeared.

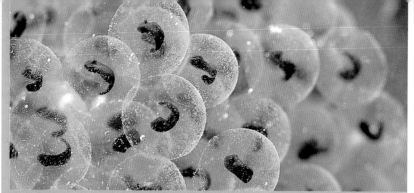
As ponds recover from acid rain damage more frogspawn is likely to survive.

# Recovering from acid rain damage

If the acid rain that causes lakes and streams to become acidic is removed, the water systems do recover. In 1999 United States scientists reported that lakes and streams across the United States and Europe appeared to be getting less acidic. However they warned that it would be decades before all the damage was reversed.

| | | |
|---|---|---|
| below pH 4.0 | | no aquatic life |
| pH 4.0 | | only frogs survive |
| pH 4.5 | | trout and bass die |
| pH 5.0 | | mayflies die, fish eggs don't survive |
| pH 5.5 | | water snails die |

## ◆ Non-sustainable solution

Acids are neutralised, or prevented from working, by mixing them with alkalis. Limestone is a naturally occurring alkali. In some of the worst affected areas, limestone is added to lakes to make them less acidic, allowing fish and other aquatic life to survive. This is a short-term, non-sustainable solution. It is very expensive and has to be repeated to prevent the water becoming acidic again. Adding limestone is certainly not an alternative to solving the cause of the problem.

Adding limestone to lakes neutralises some of the acid, but it is very expensive.

# Threat to agricultural crops

Acid rain harms many plants, not just trees. While rain that is very acidic can harm the leaves of plants, stunting their growth, most damage is caused by acid rain soaking into the soil. How well plants survive this depends on the type of plant and, more importantly, on whether the acidity stays in the soil. Sometimes it drains away or is neutralised by the soil itself.

## Acid rain on leaves

When acid rain falls on plants it damages the tough, waxy outer coating of their leaves. This damages the leaf's protection against disease, making the plant more likely to be damaged by fungi, for example. Leaves in mid growth are damaged more by acid rain than young leaves and old leaves. Damage to the outer coating of leaves can also block the stomata, the holes that allow the leaf to absorb carbon dioxide. When this happens the leaf is unable to photosynthesise as rapidly, reducing the amount of food available to the rest of the plant.

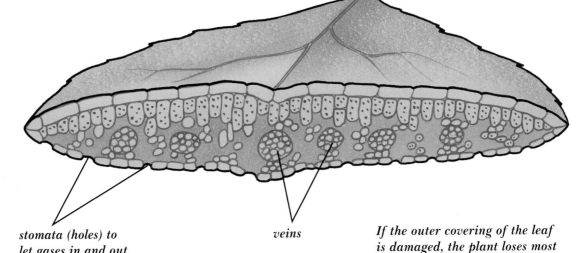

*stomata (holes) to let gases in and out*

*veins*

*If the outer covering of the leaf is damaged, the plant loses most of its protection against disease.*

# Coping with the effects of acid rain

Farmers are able to prevent many of the damaging effects of acid rain. They treat *agricultural crops* with chemicals such as lime, to neutralise the acid, and fertilisers to replace the nutrients dissolved out of the soil by the acid rain. They can also grow species or varieties of crops that are better able to cope with more acid soil.

Farmers can often use chemicals or fertilisers to reduce damage caused by acid rain.

Some plants such as cotton grass survive well in acid soils.

## Acid soil

Acid rain causes soil in some areas to become more acidic than normal. Most plants tolerate a range of acidity, but soil that is too acidic for them causes them to have weaker roots, so the whole plant is weakened and harvests are smaller. Seeds grow less well in more acid soils, so the plant does not reproduce as successfully.

# Damage to buildings

Acid rain damages stonework and makes decorative carvings very hard to see.

Acid rain affects everything it falls on, not just vegetation. Many buildings and materials show acid rain damage. Just as with human health, forests, water life and crops, the more acidic the rain, the more damage it causes.

## Acid rain on stonework

Clean rain running down stonework causes some erosion, called 'weathering'. This happens very slowly. When acidic rain falls on marble or limestone the weathering appears to happen much more quickly. This is because marble and limestone are alkaline rocks that react with the acidic rain, making it less acidic but 'using up' some of the stone. Many stone statues and decorative carvings on buildings are made of marble or limestone, because these types of stone are easy to work and pleasant to look at. Dry acid deposition also damages stonework. The famous Egyptian pyramids are being damaged by dry acid deposition.

This ancient stonework at the base of the pyramids in Giza, Egypt, has been damaged by dry acid deposition.

# Acid rain on metal

Steel and iron rust when they get damp. Rust is a type of *corrosion*, or wearing away. Most common metals used in building corrode when they get damp. Acid rain makes the corrosion happen faster, because the metal reacts with the acid to produce metal oxides. Bridges, railway lines and all other metal structures exposed to acid rain are weakened, and have to be repaired more often than if the rain was clean.

**Acid rain makes metal structures corrode more quickly than clean rain does.**

# Protection from acid rain

Most metals exposed to rain are painted to prevent corrosion. The paint prevents acid rain damaging the metal itself, but the acid rain damages the paint instead. Structures that are exposed to acid rain have to be repainted more often than if the rain were clean. Paint cannot often be used to protect decorative stonework; the stone just has to be replaced with new stone when it becomes too eroded.

**Car manufacturers use acid resistant paint for new vehicles.**

## ◆ Science in action

**What you need:** 4 small containers, distilled water, white vinegar, 2 pieces of chalk, 2 'copper' coins

Fill 2 of the containers with distilled water, and the other 2 containers with white vinegar. Place the chalk, a soft rock, in one container of vinegar and a clean, shiny 'copper' coin in the other. Place a similar coin and piece of chalk in the containers of water.

Leave them for 48 hours. What do you observe? Can you explain what has happened?

*coin in water*

*chalk in water*

*coin in vinegar*

*chalk in vinegar*

The amount of acid rain pollution varies around the world. Some countries produce much more acid rain than others. Patterns of industrial activity, prevailing winds, climates and soil types mean that different countries suffer different amounts of acid rain damage.

The areas shown in red are those that produce most acid rain pollution.

The areas shown in blue are those that scientists know have been harmed by acid rain.

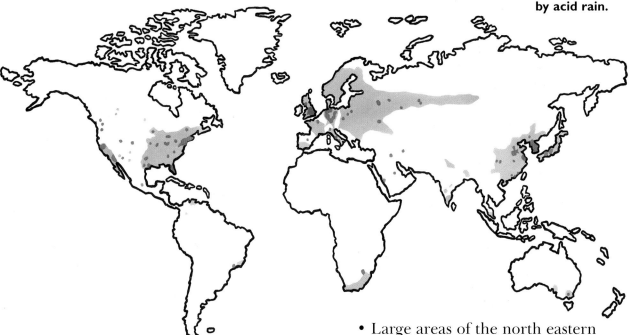

## Which areas of the world are most affected?

It is not easy to know the exact effect of acid rain around the world because some areas have been studied much more than others. However, in areas that have been studied, scientists have found the effects are widespread.

• In 1984 almost half the trees in some forests in Central Europe were showing acid rain damage.

• Large areas of the north eastern United States have soils and lakes that are so damaged as to cause lower productivity in forestry, fisheries and agriculture.

• In 2001 Environment Canada's website reported that over 80% of Canadians live in areas with 'high acid rain-related' pollution problems. Damage caused by acid rain is thought to cost $1 billion a year in Canada.

• Scientists believe that 40% of China was damaged by acid rain during the rapid industrial growth of the 1990s.

• Acid rain damage causes serious threats to human health and agriculture in about 15% of the former Soviet Union.

# International cooperation

In the 1970s scientists began studying the problem of acid rain. They rapidly realised that it was not just one country's problem. In fact, the countries most affected by acid rain problems were not always the countries causing the problems. This led to different countries working together.

Scientists from different countries share the results of their research with each other. Politicians from different countries work together to find solutions that will work for all countries. Beginning to find solutions has taken a long time. Scientists have had to find out exactly what environmental damage is caused by acid rain, and what is caused by something else. Politicians had to find solutions that would work and that shared the cost fairly between the different countries.

**Scientists around the world are working together to solve the probem of acid rain.**

## ◆ How you can help

Choose items carefully when you go shopping. A lot of fuel is used to make unnecessary plastic packaging. By buying articles with only the packaging they need you will be solving many environmental problems – and saving money too! When your family buys large items like washing machines or cars, ask them to find out which ones use least energy or use the cleanest fuel.

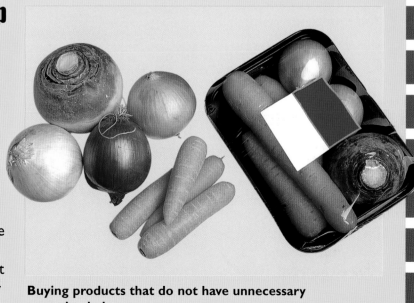

**Buying products that do not have unnecessary wrapping helps save energy**

# The solution so far

Attempts to limit the damage caused by acid rain, and eventually to repair the damage, started in the late 1970s and early 1980s. Scientists predicted that without these attempts, the problem of acid rain would worsen by as much as 50% in the next 50 years. Efforts have concentrated on controlling and reducing the production of the two main causes of acid rain, sulphur dioxide and nitrogen oxides.

## Controlling nitrogen oxides

Governments have concentrated on controlling the amount of nitrogen oxides emitted, or given out, by motor vehicles. All petrol and diesel engines emit some nitrogen oxides but engines that are old or badly maintained give out most. Since the 1980s and 1990s there have been controls on the amount of nitrogen oxides vehicles are allowed to emit, and vehicles have been tested annually. Vehicles that emit too much fail the test, and have to be improved before they can be driven again.

Vehicle emission tests control the amount of polluting gases that vehicles are allowed to give out.

# Controlling sulphur dioxide

Most sulphur dioxide comes from burning coal. Sulphur is present in coal as an impurity, an unneeded extra that doesn't burn. When the coal is burned the sulphur is given off and reacts with the air to form sulphur dioxide.

There are three ways to control the amount of sulphur dioxide in the atmosphere, and they are all used in different places. Firstly, power stations can burn 'purer' coal that contains less sulphur. Secondly, 'scrubbers' can be fixed to power stations that chemically remove the sulphur from the waste gases. Finally, we can build power stations that use a different fuel, often natural gas. This is only a short-term solution, however, as it is estimated that supplies will only last 30 or 40 years. The best long-term solution is nuclear power.

## ◆ Sustainable solution

Since the 1980s European and United States governments have been making laws to control the amount of sulphur dioxide and nitrogen oxide produced. Scientists continue to monitor the activities that produce these gases and research ways of reducing them further. They monitor the effect of acid rain on the environment and advise governments on how effective the existing laws are, and whether they need changing.

**Nuclear power stations do not burn coal, and so do not add to the problem of acid rain. However, nuclear energy produces waste that is very dangerous in other ways.**

# What about the future?

We can all help reduce the acid rain problem. Insulating our houses means it takes less energy to heat them.

Many places have been damaged by acid rain. However, in the last 20 years the situation has improved in many areas. Whether the problem of acid rain can be solved completely, and the damage undone, will depend on what governments and industries do. Individuals can help too, if they make sensible choices about the things they buy and the things they do.

## Alternative energy

*Alternative energy sources,* that do not burn fossil fuels, do not give off the chemicals that cause acid rain. Energy sources that would solve the acid rain problem include nuclear power, solar power, hydropower, geothermal energy and wind energy. At first, most of these alternative fuel sources were more expensive than fossil fuels. However, the cost of wind power has now fallen below that of fossil fuels.

Alternative energy sources, such as hydroelectric power, do not cause acid rain.

# Acid rain and global warming

A recent report by some scientists suggests that attempts to reduce acid rain may be making global warming worse. Global warming is the gradual warming up of the Earth. It is caused by extra carbon dioxide gas in the atmosphere stopping heat from Earth getting back into space. It is possible that sulphur dioxide and nitrogen oxide actually reflect some of the Sun's energy back into space, helping slow down the rate of global warming. Other scientists are not sure if this is true, or what to do about it if it is. More research may provide the answers.

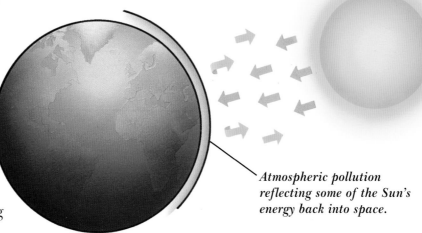

*Atmospheric pollution reflecting some of the Sun's energy back into space.*

**Some scientists believe that acid rain pollution may help prevent global warming.**

## ◆ How you can help

Reducing the amount of fossil fuel that industry burns reduces the emission of the gases that cause acid rain. You can help reduce acid rain by recycling as much rubbish as possible, such as glass, paper, aluminium and steel. It uses less fossil fuel to recycle these materials than to make new supplies from raw materials.

**Every time you recycle some of your rubbish you are helping reduce the amount of acid rain.**

## Government action

The United States Environmental Protection Agency has an Acid Rain Program that aims to steadily lower the amounts of sulphur dioxide and nitrogen oxide given out. They estimate that by 2010, when the Acid Rain Program reductions are all in place, $50 billion a year will be saved from the decrease in health problems alone. Many countries throughout the world have agreed to new laws meaning that in 2010 these countries will give out less than half the sulphur dioxide and nitrogen oxide that they did in 1980.

## There are websites where you can find out more about topics mentioned in this book.

The 'Learn.co.uk' website from 'The Guardian' has links to other websites that may be of interest to both teachers and students. It can be found at **www.learn.co.uk/primary/ environment/**

The Environment Canada website **www.ec.gc.ca/ acidrain** is an easy to use website with a 'Kids' Corner' explaining aspects of acid rain in a clear, simple, yet detailed manner.

The site **www.soton.ac.uk/ ~engenvir/environment/ air/acid.how.big.problem. html** is a site that gives simple, straightforward information.

More information about the Forest Stewardship Council can be found at **http://fscus.org/**

You can also check out **www.globalwarming.com**. It is the website of an environmental protection group dedicated to saving the Earth's natural resources and ending environmental pollution.

The United States Environmental Protection Agency website **www.epa. gov/airmarkets/acidrain** will probably be of more interest to slightly older students. It has a lot of detailed information about the causes of acid rain, what effects it has and how to measure it. It also has information on how to reduce acid rain, together with science experiments and learning activities.

The Environment Australia website **www.ea.gov.au** offers up-to-date information on the latest environmental research and initiatives. There are pages on many different topics including the greenhouse effect and pollution.

For general environmental information, you can visit the Greenpeace website at **www.greenpeace.co.uk**. To find out about the organisation's environmental campaigns in Australia, check out **www.greenpeace.org.au**.

# Glossary

## Acid deposition
The scientific name for acid rain. Wet acid deposition is acidic rain, snow or fog. Dry acid deposition is dry particles and gases.

## Agricultural crops
Plants that are grown to provide food for humans or domestic animals.

## Alternative energy sources
Types of fuel other than fossil fuels (like coal, oil, gas). Electricity made by burning fossil fuels is not an alternative energy source.

## Aquatic life
Any plants or animals that live in water, such as rivers, lakes or streams. The aquatic life affected by acid rain is freshwater life, not sea life.

## Corrosion
When water or acid causes chemical changes to a metal. For example, corrosion turns iron into rust.

## Environmental damage
Any harm to the living things in an area, or harm to the things that the living plants and animals need to survive.

## Erosion
The wearing away of rock by water or wind. Acid rain wears rock away more quickly than normal rain.

## Fossil fuels
Fuels made out of the remains of living things from millions of years ago. Coal, oil and natural gas are all fossil fuels.

## High altitude
Trees and plants at high altitude are those that are growing on the top of hills and mountains, a long way above sea level.

## Indicator solution
A special solution that changes colour when it is mixed with something acidic or alkaline. It can be used to tell how acidic soil or rainwater is.

## Industry
Factories that use machinery to make things, or power stations that make electricity for others to use. Most industries use fossil fuels, or electricity made from fossil fuels.

## Nutrients
The minute amounts of different chemicals that plants need as 'food'.

## pH numbers
Used to tell scientists how strong an acid or alkali is. A strong acid has a low pH number. Something with a pH number 7 is neutral (not acid or alkali).

## Rural areas
Areas that are mostly farms or unused countryside, with hardly any towns or industries.

## Temperature inversion
A special weather pattern where the warm air near Earth is trapped under a slightly warmer layer higher up.

## Toxic substances
Any chemicals or materials that are poisonous to plants or animals. A substance that is toxic to some living things may be harmless to others.

# Index